Becoming a Woman of Character

Freedom Series
Volume 1

Sherry Poundstone

Unless otherwise indicated, all Scripture quotations in this volume are from the New Living Translation.

©2011 FOCUS International – A Ministry for Women (Bethesda Reno-Tahoe)
ISBN-13:978-1515122586

Requests for information should be directed to
FOCUS International
info@focuswomen.org
www.focuswomen.org
775-657-8413

Becoming a Woman of Character
Table of Contents

Dear Reader,

Welcome to *Becoming a Woman of Character* Bible Study.

Whether you have been following Christ for many years or just a few days, I believe that this study on character will be of benefit to you. This 12 week study is designed for the individual or small group.

Each lesson contains a lesson, followed by questions designed to help you live out the teaching through practical application.

The suggested format for this study is to read through the lesson completely, and then re-read for more insight. Answer the *Live it Out* questions and then follow the *Prayer Points*. Allow yourself plenty of time to really dig in and meditate on each of the scriptures listed with each lesson. If you need to come back to this section at another time, be sure to make an appointment with yourself to do just that.

When we commit a verse to memory, it will be there for us to pull on when needed. I suggest choosing one verse out of each list to memorize.

Bless you on your journey to *Becoming a Woman of Character.*

Sherry Poundstone

Steps to Study

1. Purposely set aside time. Make an appointment to study *Becoming a Woman of Character*. If you are in a small group, that will be the day and time you gather with other women. If you are working through this study on your own, try to set the same day and time for your study each week. Consistency is the key.

2. Prepare to study. Select a place or a room in your house where you can be alone. Somewhere you are comfortable and at peace. This may require some creativity if you are the mom of small children or have an active household. Perhaps a local coffee place or a park might work well for you. Design it to fit your life.

3. Have all your materials available. Have your Bible, your *Becoming a Woman of Character* book, and a journal or notebook. Access to a Bible dictionary or concordance will be helpful. This can be online if that works best for you. There are many online options. One of my favorites is www.biblegateway.com

4. Prepare your heart. Talk to God about things you may need to confess, and enter your study time peacefully and without anything that may block you from receiving revelation during your study.

Lesson One
What is Character? Does it Matter?

I wasn't concerned with character as I grew up. I was concerned with survival.

I'm not even sure that I heard the word character in my family at all. Most likely I heard about character in school, but I don't remember ever wondering if I had it.

I grew up in the conservative Midwest, and at a time when family dysfunction of any kind was not talked about. My extended family was one plagued by alcohol, drug, sexual and physical abuse; all stemming from physical depression and spiritual oppression. What I now know to be a spirit of lying, had invaded my family and permeated every nook and cranny of our home. It was actually a dangerous place for a little girl, but as often is the case, no one on the outside knew.

I gave my life to Jesus Christ at age 14 and right then I made the decision to be different; to purpose to live a life without financial struggle, emotional pain, abuse or heartbreak. Unfortunately, I took the long way around in getting to the life I so desired. I had no idea how to accomplish this life and what I did not understand at the time, was I did not have the character to support a different lifestyle. My character was weak.

My early adult life was earmarked with common mistakes made by a woman growing up in an abusive environment.

I found myself choosing the "wrong" man and then fighting to keep him. I struggled with every area of my life: romantic relationships, financial responsibility and interpersonal skills.

I want to make it clear that I am not placing blame on my parents. Once we are adults, and once we know different, we can make the choice for a better life. My point here is only to show that I lacked character in a big way and why.

What is Character?

Abraham Lincoln said "Character, is like a tree and reputation like its shadow. The shadow is what we think of it; the tree is the real thing."

Webster defines character as "a moral or ethical quality: Our moral state", and that is true. But as women following Christ, is there more?

Character is much more than what others see on the outside. It has been said that character is *who we are when no one is looking*, or when there is no one around to judge us, to give us a pat on the back, or give us recognition.

Through God's word, we can come to know His character. His love, mercy, and compassion; His courage and strength; His faithfulness and justice.

As Christ followers, we want our character to match up with who we say we are. We want to develop and display the character of strong, Christ centered women.

Dale Carnegie said *"Be more concerned with your character than your reputation, because your character is what you really are, while your reputation is merely what others think you are."*

So what does it mean to become a woman of character? A woman of character means living from a point of authenticity. A woman of character is honest, full of integrity, reliable, loyal, forgiving, kind, and compassionate.

We must seek character traits which reflect Christ in us. God's word makes it very clear what Christian character traits we are to have. As Christ followers this is our guideline.

But the Holy Spirit produces this kind of fruit in our lives: love, joy, peace, patience, kindness, goodness, faithfulness......Galatians 5:22

Does Character Matter?

Susan and Mary had been friends for years. Susan thought she knew Mary to be a woman of character. That's why she was shocked and disappointed to find out that Mary was having an extramarital affair with a co-worker. When confronted, Mary gave every excuse to justify the affair. She expected that her friendship with Susan would continue on as always. Susan could choose to end the relationship, or, she could choose to stand by her friend as she worked through the situation. A woman of character could choose to stand by Mary and help her through repentance and restoration.

A few years ago, during a presidential election, one candidate's theme was "Character Matters". The idea was to get Americans thinking about the character of the candidates, as well as their political stance and ideas. Since character is defined as our moral state, then a candidate's character should matter to us.

Does character matter? Character matters to God! If it wasn't important to the Lord there wouldn't be so much instruction in His word regarding character. When God places an emphasis on something we need to pay attention!

Becoming a woman of character may be challenging and, at times, even difficult. There are many influences from society that do not support being a woman of character. What is acceptable in our American culture today doesn't reflect biblical values or God's instruction. We see that cheating, irresponsibility, a self-focused attitude, and a relaxation of moral values is acceptable by many. We must purpose to take a stand for what is right and the first step is to become women of character.

Where Do We Start?

We must *choose* to become women of strong character. This means we should allow God to work in our lives to develop our character and strengthen us in areas where we are weak. Let's look at the steps we should take.

1. Choose to pursue the process of becoming a woman of character.

For just as the heavens are higher than the earth, so my ways are higher than your ways and my thoughts higher than your thoughts. Isaiah 55:9

Free will allows us to choose the path we are going to follow. Will we take the easy way out and follow the world's ways? Or will we turn toward God and make the choices He wants us to follow? We face many free will choices every day. But God's ways are higher than our ways and His thoughts are higher than our thoughts.

2. Get humble before the Lord.

Remember how the LORD your God led you through the wilderness for these forty years, humbling you and testing you to prove your character, and to find out whether or not you would obey his commands. Deuteronomy 8:2

The Lord tested the children of Israel in the wilderness for forty years. He humbled them and tested their character. As women of character, we must humble ourselves before God and search our hearts. Are we willing to remain humble in all areas of our life? To allow God to teach us the meaning of true character and allow Him to make changes in us?

3. Change Our Thinking

Don't copy the behavior and customs of this world, but let God transform you into a new person by changing the way you think. Then you will learn to know God's will for you, which is good and pleasing and perfect. Romans 12:2

We must change our thinking if we are to become women of character. Changing our thinking will change our behavior. I like to think of this equation: Thoughts=words=actions=outcomes

Our thoughts become our words. We never speak anything that we haven't thought about first. Our words become our actions. Our actions always produce an outcome, good or bad. The outcome reflects our character.

An example that I often use is when we make a *free will* choice to gossip.

4. Allow God to Work

"I am the true grapevine, and my Father is the gardener. He cuts off every branch of mine that doesn't produce fruit, and he prunes the branches that do bear fruit so they will produce even more. John 15:1-2

The pruning process is hard! It hurts. But it is through this process that we will reach our goal of being women of character. We must allow God to trim and prune anything that He doesn't want in us, and to replace what He pruned with His character.

Live It Out

1. What does character mean to you?

2. What is the difference between character and reputation? How can the two be confused?

3. Think of a person that you believe has character. What traits do you see in the person that makes you believe he/she has character?

4. What are some temptations or distractions that could get in the way of becoming a woman of character?

Prayer Points

Pray and ask God to help you choose to become a woman of character. Humble yourself before the Lord and ask Him to reveal any areas of your character that need development. Then ask for His guidance as you begin to develop these areas to reflect Christ's character.

Further Study

The following scriptures give us a picture of the character of Christ. Read through each of these verses and ponder their meaning. How can you apply these verses to your life?

John 13:1-5
Ephesians 5:1-2
Colossians 3:13
I Peter 1:15-16
John 3:7
Ephesians 4:32
I John 3:3

Choose one verse to commit to memory.

Lesson 2
Building Character Through Integrity

Better is a poor man who walks in his integrity than a rich man who is crooked in his ways. Proverbs 28:6

Betty was on the women's ministry staff at her local church and therefore spent many hours with the Pastor Thomas' wife. They worked side by side planning events, attending Bible studies and working in the community. Betty had many opportunities to observe Mrs. Thomas in various settings and with different people. After awhile, Betty began to notice that Mrs. Thomas' demeanor changed depending on the people she was with. If she were in the presence of the elder's wives, she was positive, encouraging and supportive. If she was giving instruction to church volunteers, she was often bossy, sarcastic and frustrated with them. Worse yet, was Mrs. Thomas' dishonoring behavior toward her husband. Do you think Mrs. Thomas was a woman of integrity?

Integrity is the quality of being complete or undivided. Webster defines integrity as "the state of being complete or whole."
A woman of integrity is the same person in all situations. She is the same person at home as she is at work, at church or out with friends. This quality is very important in building character because the consistency of behavior builds trust. If we know that each and every time we have an interaction with someone we can expect them to be the same, trust can be built.

Have you ever heard the saying that your life may be the only Bible some people read, or the only Jesus they may ever see? People want to know that integrity really exists. In our world today, there are many examples of people who are not the same in every situation. People who change the way speak and act depending on who they are around. Do you know people like that?

As women of God, we should be separate from the world, but we are not to have a superior attitude, or have an attitude that everyone else is "less than."
We are called to be separate in our character, and as Christ followers we should be women of integrity.

Integrity is doing the right thing for the right reason, but it does not mean being perfect. It means that we are striving to be the same everywhere we go. It means that when we make mistakes, we can be transparent and open about it, repent, be forgiven and move on.

Read through the Book of Ruth. In Chapter 1, we see that Ruth was a woman of strong character and integrity. She displayed these traits through her loyalty to her mother-in-law Naomi, as well as through her hard work in the Boaz's fields. Her integrity and strong character were rewarded. Ruth and Naomi came to Bethlehem poor but became prosperous through Ruth's marriage to Boaz. God rewarded her integrity, her character.

Consider the following account and example of integrity:

Lt. John Blanchard was a young soldier stationed at an Army Base in Florida during the first part of WWII. One day he was reading through a book he had borrowed from the Base Library. He was impressed with some of the notes written in the margin. They were written in feminine handwriting and they were so tender and so thought provoking that he looked back at the fly-leaf to see who had been the previous owner of the book. He found it was a woman named Hollis Maynell.

Blanchard did some research and found her address in New York. He wrote her a letter telling her how much he appreciated her insights in the book. The next day he was shipped overseas but for the next thirteen months, John Blanchard and Hollis Maynell corresponded back and forth. They developed a tremendous relationship through their correspondence and found they had much in common and they thought very much alike.

They began to realize they were falling in love with each other though they had never met. Blanchard asked Hollis Maynell if she would send a picture but she refused. She wrote, "If you really care about me, it wouldn't matter what I look like because its character and what's inside that really counts."

After thirteen months the day finally came when he was to meet her. They made arrangements to meet at Grand Central Station in New York City at 7:00 p.m. on a particular night. She said, "You'll be able to identify me by the red rose I'll be wearing in my lapel."

Lt. Blanchard waited with anticipation. Finally, a group of people got off a train and were coming toward him. Out in front was a slender, blond woman with great poise and beauty. She came in a pale green dress that looked like the freshness of spring and his heart leaped out of his chest as he started toward her.

Then he saw that she did not have a red rose in her lapel even though she was looking directly at him. As she went by with a provocative smile she said, "Going my way, soldier?" Suddenly, he felt a strong desire to follow her but then right behind her he saw Hollis Maynell. She was over forty years of age, had graying hair and was vastly overweight but she was wearing a rose in the lapel of her wrinkled coat. She had gray eyes and a kindly expression but he was so disappointed.

Everything within him wanted to chase after the beautiful blond who was now disappearing. But then he remembered the relationship he developed through those letters and even though this probably wouldn't develop into marriage, he realized maybe it would develop into something very meaningful, a friendship, and a companionship perhaps that he had not known before. So, without hesitation, he handed her the book which identified him to her and reached for her bag and said, "Are you ready to go to dinner?"

"Young man, I don't know what this is all about," she said, "but that blond woman begged me to put on this red rose and she said if you asked me out to eat with you I should tell you that you were suppose to meet her in the restaurant across the street. She said it was some kind of test."

Lt. John Blanchard passed the test. Would you?

Becoming a woman of character involves being a woman of integrity. Decide today to be the same person with everyone you are with, in every situation.

Live It Out

1. *People with integrity walk safely, but those who follow crooked paths will be exposed.* Proverbs 10:9 What does this scripture mean to you?

2. What does being a woman of integrity mean regarding relationships?

   Marriage:

   Parenting:

   Friendship:

   Co-Workers:

3. Think of a situation where to keep your word (your commitment) would be an imposition. How did you handle it?

4. Proverbs 2:7-8 tells us that our integrity will protect us. What do you think that means, and what does it look like in everyday life?

Prayer Points:
Ask the Lord to help you in your pursuit of integrity. Pray for God to reveal areas of your life you may need to change. As He reveals these areas, begin to take action to make those changes.

Further Study:
Read the following scriptures and think of examples in your own life for each one. What lessons have you learned from these experiences?

Proverbs 11:3
Proverbs 28:6
1 Peter 3:16
Proverbs 12:22
Proverbs 21:3
2 Corinthians 8:21
John 14:6
Proverbs 4:25-27
Hebrews 13:18

Choose one verse to commit to memory.

Lesson 3
Building Character Through Honesty

Lying lips are an abomination to the LORD, but those who act faithfully are his delight. Proverbs 12:22

Christine wanted the promotion to district sales manager more than anything. She had the experience and training, but she did not have the advanced degree required for the position. She knew she could perform the duties of district sales manager better than any other candidate. At first, she dismissed the idea of claiming she had the necessary education when she didn't. But the more she thought about it, the more it seemed harmless to lie about having the degree. After all, what would it matter once she was secure in the position and helping the company meet its sales goals? Christine thought that the Human Resources department would most likely not verify her degree, because she was well liked and very successful within the company and they trusted her. The more she thought about it, the easier it became to lie.

If no one ever finds out, is it okay to lie?

Webster defines honesty as "honorable; characterized by integrity and straightforwardness in conduct, in thought and in speech; free from fraud; genuine, fully unadulterated; open; frank; sincere."

A woman of character is honest. When we live a life of honesty, we are trusted.

There are six things the LORD *hates— no, seven things he detests: haughty eyes, a lying tongue, hands that kill the innocent, a heart that plots evil, feet that race to do wrong, a false witness who pours out lies, a person who sows discord in a family.* Proverbs 6:16-19

Cheating and dishonesty are running rampant in our society today. In April 2014, ABC Primetime News published an online article. Here are some very revealing excerpts from that article.

- Authoritative numbers are hard to come by, but according to a 2002 confidential survey of 12,000 high school students, 74 percent admitted cheating on an examination at least once in the past year.

- In a six-month investigation, Primetime travelled to colleges and high schools across the country to see how students are cheating, and why. The bottom line is not just that many students have more temptation — but they seem to have a whole new mindset.

- Joe is a student at a top college in the Northeast who admits to cheating regularly. Like all of the college students who spoke to Primetime, he wanted his identity obscured. In Joe's view, he's just doing what the rest of the world does. "The real world is terrible," he told Gibson. "People will take other people's materials and pass it on as theirs. I'm numb to it already. I'll cheat to get by."

This information is disturbing and reflects how our society views being dishonest as not only acceptable, but a necessity to compete.

But honesty is more than telling the truth. It is being honest with God, ourselves and others. It's honouring the Lord by not attempting to deceive Him (as if we could!).

Where do we begin to develop the character trait of honesty?

We must be honest with God. God is all-knowing so it's not like He doesn't already know what's going on with us. But He wants us to be honest with Him. When in prayer, He wants us to talk to Him about our emotions and feelings. We should confess our sins and repent. He wants us to talk to Him about our life issues.

We must be honest with ourselves. God wants us to accept who we are in Him and live as our true selves, rather than trying to live according to other people's expectations.

We must be honest with others. Don't lie! Be truthful with your husband, children, family, friends and co-workers. Be known as a woman of character who tells the truth and can be trusted.

So what can get in the way of being an honest woman? The desire for money, self- promotion, title or position can all be very enticing. But we can't let anything throw us off the honesty train. A woman of character is honest, and by being honest, she is trustworthy.

We are careful to be honourable before the Lord, but we also want everyone else to see that we are honourable. 2 Corinthians 8:21

For the Scriptures say, "If you want to enjoy life and see many happy days, keep your tongue from speaking evil and your lips from telling lies." 1Peter 3:10

And you will know the truth, and the truth will set you free. John 8:32

Don't lie to each other, for you have stripped off your old sinful nature and all its wicked deeds. Colossians 3:9

Live It Out

1. *The LORD detests lying lips, but he delights in those who tell the truth.* Proverbs 12:22. Knowing this is true, what are some things that could tempt a Christ follower into being dishonest?

2. To become a woman of character, we must be trustworthy. Name some ways we can become trustworthy with our spouse, children, friends, co-workers.

3. Think of a situation where you needed to be honest with someone. (Was your honesty more about you or the other person?) Were you honest with love and kindness or with judgment?

4. Do you believe that being dishonest with yourself is better or worse than being dishonest with others? Why?

Prayer Points

Pray and ask the Lord to reveal to you any areas of
dishonesty in your life. Repent and ask for forgiveness.
Then ask God to show you a new way of living with
honesty in all areas of your life.

Further Study

Read and meditate on the following scriptures. Take a few
minutes and write out a few that really speak to you.
Online tools, or a study bible, are a great resource for
going deeper into the word. Online options include
www.biblegateway.com or www.bibleresources.org .

Scriptures on Honesty

Proverbs 12:22
Proverbs 19:1
2 Corinthians 8:21
Proverbs 6:16-20
John 8:32
1 Peter 3:10-12
Philippians 4:8-9
Colossians 3:9
Hebrews 13:18
Proverbs 11:3
Exodus 20:16
Luke 6:31

Choose one verse to commit to memory.

Lesson 4
Building Character Through Kindness

How important is kindness? In a recent study of 37 cultures around the world, 16,000 subjects were asked about their most desired traits in a mate. For both sexes, the first preference was kindness.

As women of character, we must develop the desire to be kind. This character trait is critical in reflecting Christ in our lives.

I think most people would say kindness as going out of their way to help someone. That's true, but there's so much more! The dictionary defines kindness as: the quality of being warm-hearted and considerate and humane and sympathetic. The character trait of kindness is an important one and, in most of us, must be developed. It simply doesn't come naturally to many of us.

But the Holy Spirit produces this kind of fruit in our lives: love, joy, peace, patience, kindness, goodness, faithfulness, gentleness, and self-control. There is no law against these things! Galatians 5:22-23

Paul's definition of the Fruit of The Spirit lists kindness as the fifth fruit. This is a natural progression of the fruits. If we exhibit the first four Fruits of the Spirit, (love, joy peace and patience) we will show kindness.

Kindness must be learned. Violence and other terrible

influences in media can cause people to become desensitized toward the needs and feelings of others. Children must be taught what it is to be kind and we must pray for them to have the desire to be kind to others.

Some people believe that to display kindness is to appear weak, but it's really just the opposite. To be kind takes courage. Displaying kindness toward another person requires discipline and a determination to take the focus off ourselves.

Paul warns of an end time world without kindness in 2 Timothy, Chapter 3.

*You should know this, Timothy, that in the last days there will be very difficult times. For people will love only themselves and their money. They will be boastful and proud, scoffing at God, disobedient to their parents, and ungrateful. They will consider nothing sacred. They will be unloving and unforgiving; they will slander others and have no self-control. They will be cruel and hate what is good.*2 Timothy 3:1-3

Where Do We Start?

Keep a soft heart. We must keep our hearts soft and tender toward others and allow ourselves to feel compassion. This is often a difficult area for those of us who have been hurt in the past. But if it is a fruit of the Spirit, then it is important enough to focus on. Ask Jesus to help you keep a tender attitude and a soft, pliable heart toward others.

Look for opportunities. Watch for people and situations that the Lord places in your path that could use a word of kindness. Let's purpose to be aware and alert to the situations and needs of others.

Take action. We must decide to take action as soon as we see the need. If we hesitate, or think "I will do it later", the opportunity may vanish. Taking action will often include some kind of SELF-SACRIFICE on our part. This often is a sacrifice of our time, or an altering in our own personal schedule. Taking action may simply be speaking encouragement to someone, giving them hope and showing them they are not alone.

Dear children, let's not merely say that we love each other; let us show the truth by our actions. 1 John 3:18

"Watch out! Don't do your good deeds publicly, to be admired by others, for you will lose the reward from your Father in heaven. When you give to someone in need, don't do as the hypocrites do—blowing trumpets in the synagogues and streets to call attention to their acts of charity! I tell you the truth, they have received all the reward they will ever get. But when you give to someone in need, don't let your left hand know what your right hand is doing. Give your gifts in private, and your Father, who sees everything, will reward you. Matthew 6:1-4

We must be careful that our acts of kindness not be motivated by pride. What if every act of kindness we ever displayed was kept quiet and no one knew? Would we still be as motivated to act? Genuine kindness is lending a helping hand when you expect nothing in return.

Don't be selfish; don't try to impress others. Be humble, thinking of others as better than yourselves. Don't look out only for your own interests, but take an interest in others, too. Philippians 2:3-4

Biblical Example of Kindness

There are many biblical examples of kindness. Jesus practiced kindness that was radical for the day and time He lived in. He had great concern for all people; men, women, children, Jew and Gentile.

- King David toward Mephibosheth in 2 Samuel, Chapter 9.
- The Shunammite woman and her husband toward Elisha in 2 Kings 4:8-10.
- Dorcas in Acts 9:36-39.
- The Samaritan in Luke 10:25-37.
- Barnabas Acts 4:36.
- The Proverbs 31 woman in Proverbs 31:20.

"What is desirable in a man is his kindness, and it is better to be a poor man than a liar." Proverbs 19:22

Don't you see how wonderfully kind, tolerant, and patient God is with you? Does this mean nothing to you? Can't you see that his kindness is intended to turn you from your sin? Romans 2:4

Live It Out

1. What does kindness mean to you?

2. How is kindness connected to our character?

3. What does kindness accomplish?

4. What are some ways we can show kindness to our spouse, children, friends, co-workers?

5. Think of someone who has shown you kindness recently. In what way? How was it expressed?

6. Think of 5 acts of kindness that you can perform today.

Prayer Points

Ask God to place kindness and mercy in your heart. Take a closer look at those who have not treated you kindly or who mistreat others. Ask God to give you a merciful heart and kind attitude toward those people.

Further Study

Use the following verses on kindness to go deeper in your study. Ask the Lord to reveal to you what He wants you to see, feel and hear through these verses.

Scripture on Kindness

Ephesians 4:32
Luke 6:35
Proverbs 11:17
Colossians 3:12
Proverbs 31:26 .
1 Corinthians 13:4-7
Proverbs 19:17
1 Peter 3:9
1 John 3:18
Philippians 2:1-30
Colossians 3:14
1 Peter 4:8
1 John 3:17
Ephesians 4:29
2 Thessalonians 3:13
Matthew 5:42

Choose one verse to commit to memory.

Lesson 5
Building Character through Forgiveness

What do you think of when you hear the word forgiveness? Does it bring to mind people, places or things that hurt you? Do you get a sick feeling in your stomach thinking about how you will never forgive "so and so" for what they did?

These are common reactions until we understand forgiveness and how God instructs us in this area. The Word of Truth, God's Word, tells us exactly how to respond and what action to take.

If you forgive those who sin against you, your heavenly Father will forgive you. But if you refuse to forgive others, your Father will not forgive your sins. Matthew 6:14-15

But when you are praying, first forgive anyone you are holding a grudge against, so that your Father in heaven will forgive your sins, too. Mark 11:25-26

Is forgiveness a choice?
Yes and No. Yes. Forgiveness happens through a decision of our will in response and obedience to God and His command to forgive.

And No, because according to the scriptures, we have no choice but to forgive. The Bible instructs us to forgive as the Lord forgave us.

Make allowance for each other's faults, and forgive anyone who offends you. Remember, the Lord forgave you, so you must forgive others. Colossians 3:13

God forgives us our sins as we forgive others who have sinned against us. Adopt a lifestyle of forgiving others. Make it part of your daily prayers, make it habit.

This is a heart issue. We must be willing to lay down the offense, the hurt, the pain and the need for retribution.

What forgiveness is NOT
Forgiveness is not condoning what was done to us. When we forgive someone, we are not saying what he or she did was ok. And we are not giving them permission to repeat the offense.
Denial is not forgiveness. Forgiveness is dealing with the truth no matter how painful. Denying the facts or the incident—pretending it didn't happen, is not forgiveness. We do not need to live in the past or wallow in the offense, but we must recognize and acknowledge that it happened. Forgetting is not forgiving. However, when we forgive, we'll eventually forget or at least recall the incident without emotion.
Putting on a show is not forgiveness. In other words, saying we forgive someone when we have no intention of doing so is pretense and means nothing.

How do we forgive when we don't feel like it?
We must trust the Holy Spirit and have faith He will give us the ability to truly forgive. We forgive, by faith out of

obedience, whether we feel like it or not and have faith that the Holy Spirit will complete the work.

God honors our commitment and decision to obey Him. He sees our heart. He knows if we are sincere and if we are truly choosing to forgive. We must continue to forgive, by faith, until the work of forgiveness is done in our hearts.

And I am certain that God, who began the good work within you, will continue his work until it is finally finished on the day when Christ Jesus returns. Philippians 1:6

How will we know if we have truly forgiven?
Corrie Ten Boom, a Christian woman who survived a Nazi concentration camp during the Holocaust, said, "Forgiveness is to set a prisoner free, and to realize the prisoner was you."

We will know the work of forgiveness is complete when we experience the freedom that comes as a result. We are the ones who suffer most when we choose not to forgive. When we forgive, the Lord sets our hearts free from the anger, bitterness, resentment and hurt that previously imprisoned us. It's often a slow or gradual process, but can also be immediate.

Then Peter came to him and asked, "Lord, how often should I forgive someone who sins against me? Seven times?" "No, not seven times," Jesus replied, "but seventy times seven! Matthew 18:21-22

This answer by Jesus makes it clear that forgiveness is not easy for us. It's not a one-time choice and then we automatically live in a state of forgiveness. Forgiveness may require a lifetime of forgiving, but it is important to the Lord. We must continue forgiving until the matter is settled in our heart.

I'd like to share with you an illustration from Richard Hoefler's book, *Will Daylight Come,* of how sin enslaves and forgiveness frees.

A little boy visiting his grandparents was given his first slingshot. He practiced in the woods, but he could never hit his target. As he came back to Grandma's back yard, he spied her pet duck. On an impulse he took aim and let fly. The stone hit, and the duck fell dead.

The boy panicked. Desperately he hid the dead duck in the woodpile, only to look up and see his sister watching. Sally had seen it all, but she said nothing.

After lunch that day, Grandma said, "Sally, let's wash the dishes." But Sally said, "Johnny told me he wanted to help in the kitchen today. Didn't you, Johnny?" And she whispered to him, "Remember the duck! So Johnny did the dishes.

Later Grandpa asked if the children wanted to go fishing, Grandma said, "I'm sorry, but I need Sally to help make supper." Sally smiled and said, "That's all taken care of. Johnny wants to do it." Again she whispered, "Remember the duck." Johnny stayed while Sally went fishing.

After several days of Johnny doing both his chores and Sally's, finally he couldn't stand it. He confessed to Grandma that he'd killed the duck.

"I know, Johnny," she said, giving him a hug. "I was standing at the window and saw the whole thing. Because I love you, I forgave you. I wondered how long you would let Sally make a slave of you.

How long will un-forgiveness make a slave of you?

What does it look like to forgive? Must we contact the offender in person, or by email or phone? Must we be friends? Must we carry on as if nothing happened? Do I have to tell the offender its okay?
We must be humble and admit that we have un-forgiveness toward a person.

Humble yourselves before the Lord, and he will lift you up in honor. James 4:10

So humble yourselves under the mighty power of God, and at the right time he will lift you up in honor. 1Peter 5:6

Choose to forgive the offender.

"If you forgive those who sin against you, your heavenly Father will forgive you. Matthew 6:14

Forgive often and forgive without conditions. Often the person doesn't know they have offended you so forgiveness is not dependent on an apology or an admission from the other.

Give up the idea of avenging the offense.

Don't say, "I will get even for this wrong." Wait for the LORD *to handle the matter.* Proverbs 20:22

Pray for the Lord to reveal ALL TRUTH.
Then you will know the truth, and the truth will set you free." John 8:32
Ask God to show you the truth about yourself and all involved.

Pray and take the Lord's hand.

Again---*Humble yourselves before the Lord, and he will lift you up in honor.* James 4:10

Take action if the Lord instructs you to do so.

If God instructs you to forgive someone through a letter, email or text, then you must do it. But this isn't always the case. The person might not know you are offended or hurt and their reaction might bring more offense. Forgiving someone is ultimately between you and God. Pursue any un-forgiveness in your life and begin to forgive.

Live It Out

1. When you hear the word forgiveness, what emotions, thoughts or words come to mind?

2. How is the willingness to forgive connected to our character?

3. How does the popular saying "drinking poison and expecting the other person to die" pertain to forgiveness?

4. Is forgiveness a choice? Why?

5. Why is it important to God that we forgive others?

Prayer Points/Further Study

Ask the Lord to show you any areas of un-forgiveness in your life then follow these guidelines to forgive the people involved.

1. Humble yourself before the Lord, and acknowledge the offense.
2. Choose to forgive.
3. Give up "avenging" the offense.
4. Pray for God to reveal all truth about the situation.
5. Take the Lord's hand and allow Him to lift you out of the pit!
6. Take further action ONLY at the Lord's instruction.

Read and meditate on the following verses. Using your bible or online tools, look up at least 10 additional scriptures on forgiveness.

Matthew 6:14-15
Colossians 3:13
Ephesians 4:31-32
Matthew 18: 21-22
2 Corinthians 2:5-8
1 Corinthians 13:4-6
Matthew 5:23-24
Luke 6:37
John 8:7
Acts 7:59-60
Luke 23:33-34

Choose one verse to commit to memory.

Lesson 6
Building Character through Image

A woman of character knows who she is in Christ. The image of her life, reflected back to her, is a woman who God created.

How we see ourselves influences how we see others. How we see others is a reflection of our character. In other words, if we are women of character we will see others, and ourselves, as God created us.

The Webster dictionary says the definition of self-image is "the idea, conception, or mental image one has of oneself." Our self-image is often measured by the world's false standards: material success (money and possessions), intelligence, talents, or what others think of us.

Determining self-image by your money and possessions can create a false security.

Proverbs 11:28 says *" Trust in your money and down you go! But the godly flourish like leaves in spring."*

In Matthew we read about how the rich young ruler's love of his possessions kept him from following Jesus.

Someone came to Jesus with this question: "Teacher, what good deed must I do to have eternal life?" "Why ask me about what is good?" Jesus replied. "There is only One who is good. But to answer your question—if you want to receive eternal life, keep the commandments." "Which ones?" the man asked. And Jesus replied: "You must not murder. You must not commit adultery. You must not steal. You must not testify falsely. Honor your father and mother. Love your neighbor as yourself." "I've obeyed all these commandments," the young man replied. "What else must I do?" Jesus told him, "If you want to be perfect, go and sell all your possessions and give the money to the poor, and you will have treasure in heaven. Then come, follow me." But when the young man heard this, he went away sad, for he had many possessions.

Matthew 19:16-22

Who we are, and who God created us to be, has nothing to do with our money, status or possessions.

All intelligence comes from God. We must be careful not to allow it to determine our self-image.

God is the source of our intelligence. If we don't realize this, it would be easy to take credit and revel in the praise and glory it can bring. Instead, we must praise God for the gift of intelligence and the opportunities to learn and grow.

All talents and abilities are a gift from God.

How can we boast or allow our self-image to be tied up in something we did not earn but received as a gift?

Do you have the gift of speaking? Then speak as though God himself were speaking through you. Do you have the gift of helping others? Do it with all the strength and energy that God supplies. Then everything you do will bring glory to God through Jesus Christ. All glory and power to him forever and ever! Amen. 1Peter 4:11

We have a responsibility to steward well the gifts and abilities God has bestowed on us, but we must not allow these gifts to determine our identity.

The opinion of others must not determine our self-image.

Many people did believe in him, however, including some of the Jewish leaders. But they wouldn't admit it for fear that the Pharisees would expel them from the synagogue. For they loved human praise more than the praise of God. John 12:42-43

These verses point out that man's opinion of us should not determine our self image. We are not to believe what others say about who we are, but rather know what God says about who we are. How we see ourselves is important to God. God wants us to know who we are in Him and how He created us. We are created in HIS image.

So God created man in His own image; in the image of God He created him; male and female He created them. Genesis 1:27

And the Lord God formed man of the dust of the ground, and breathed into his nostrils the breath of life; and man became a living being. Genesis 2:7

So how does God see us?
God sees us as acceptable. *Because of his grace he declared us righteous and gave us confidence that we will inherit eternal life.* Titus 3:7

God sees us as lovable. Not only are we acceptable, but we are also lovable.

For this is how God loved the world: He gave his one and only Son, so that everyone who believes in him will not perish but have eternal life. John 3:16

God sees us as capable. *It is not that we think we are qualified to do anything on our own. Our qualification comes from God. He has enabled us to be ministers of his new covenant. This is a covenant not of written laws, but of the Spirit. The old written covenant ends in death; but under the new covenant, the Spirit gives life.*
2Corinthians 3:5-6

We are acceptable, lovable and capable in God's eyes. Focus on that truth. Study the word, stay in prayer and do not listen to anything else!

Live It Out

1. What kinds of influences determine your self-image? (Are there certain people, situations, times or places in which your self-image is affected?)

2. Do you feel that you are allowing the "world" to determine your self-image? How? (Be specific so that you can take this issue to the Lord in prayer.)

3. God see us as acceptable (Titus 3:7). Is it difficult or easy for you to see yourself this way? Why?

4. Do you feel lovable? Do you believe God sees you this way? What is the truth?

5. How can we help our spouse and children see themselves as God sees them? List some specific ways.

Prayer Points

Write out a prayer asking God to help you change from measuring your self-image by the world's standards to His standards, to know you are created in His image.

Further Study
Read the following verses. These verses will give further meaning on the attributes of God and how he created us.
Judges 5:11
Ezra 9:15
Job 36:3
Genesis 18:20, 21, 25,
Exodus 20:5
Exodus 34:7
John 3:16
Romans 5:8-10
 Romans 8:37-39
 1 John 4:9-11
Deuteronomy 32:4
2 Samuel 22:31
Psalm 18:30
Matthew 5:48
Romans 12:2

Choose one verse to commit to memory.

Lesson 7
Building Character Through Serving

For you have been called to live in freedom, my brothers and sisters. But don't use your freedom to satisfy your sinful nature. Instead, use your freedom to serve one another in love. Galatians 5:13

A woman of character serves the Lord by serving others.

In times when you feel discouraged, depressed or your circumstances seem hopeless, serve someone! Find someone to help. It will change everything for you. Get the focus off your problems and onto another person in need of something: a ride to church, food, an encouraging word, or maybe a listening ear. SERVE someone else.

In other words, it's not about you or me. It's about Jesus. It's about serving Him by serving others. It may not always be the guy on the street holding a sign. Instead, it may be the woman sitting next to you in church who appears to have everything she needs but is experiencing a trial.

God gave us gifts, talents and abilities to be used by serving others. They are not for our benefit. We were put here to serve God, and the way we serve God is by serving other people.

God has given each of you a gift from his great variety of spiritual gifts. Use them well to serve one another. 1 Peter 4:10

So how do we move ourselves out of the way and serve God by serving others?

Be available and willing to serve.
Never tell your neighbors to wait until tomorrow if you can help them now. Proverbs 3:28
You may be out of your comfort zone; you may have something else planned. But we are the hands and feet of Jesus on this earth. How did Jesus handle this type of situation? Let's look at Matthew 20:30-32:

Two blind men were sitting beside the road. When they heard that Jesus was coming that way, they began shouting, "Lord, Son of David, have mercy on us!" "Be quiet!" the crowd yelled at them. But they only shouted louder, "Lord, Son of David, have mercy on us!" When Jesus heard them, he stopped and called, "What do you want me to do for you?"

Don't look out only for your own interests, but take an interest in others, too. Philippians 2:4

What gets in the way of us being willing to serve? In a word, we can be selfish. Any time we encounter someone with a need; it is God giving us the opportunity to learn to serve, to learn and to be like Jesus Christ. Our busy lives can actually block our compassion for others. "I am too busy to serve" is a common statement I hear from the women I counsel.

Farmers who wait for perfect weather never plant. If they watch every cloud, they never harvest. Ecclesiastes 11:4

Don't wait for the perfect time or circumstance to begin to serve because most likely, you never will. It's not often that everything lines up in the perfect way to serve.

Be thankful and glad to serve.
Worship the LORD with gladness. Come before him, singing with joy. Psalm 100:4
If we stay in a state of thankfulness and worship, we will want to serve others. This can become a lifestyle for us, a habit.

If we remember what Jesus did for us on the cross, we will stay thankful and want to serve others.

 I love how The Message Bible says it:
This is how much God loved the world: He gave his Son, his one and only Son. And this is why: so that no one need be destroyed; by believing in him, anyone can have a whole and lasting life. John 3:16

At times, we can be judgmental of others and this can get in the way of us being thankful.

"Who are you to condemn someone else's servants? Their own master will judge whether they stand or fall. And with the Lord's help, they will stand and receive his approval." Romans 14:4

Comparison or criticism of others can become a wall that prevents us from staying thankful. Holding on to offense, bitterness and envy can also get in the way of our thankfulness.

Serve with the right motive.
Watch out! Don't do your good deeds publicly, to be admired by others, for you will lose the reward from your Father in heaven. Matthew 6:1

Self-promotion and servant hood don't mix. It's important that we ask ourselves why we are serving. Are we serving to get people to like us? To obtain a position? To be seen or noticed? Are we striking a deal with God (I will do this if You will do that)? Any self promotion is wrong. We need to be honest with ourselves about that.

In my years of counseling women, I have seen many cases where serving for the wrong reason created an offense. For example, I have seen many women commit to serving in an area in order to obtain favor with church leadership. And I've seen it backfire! When the position, title or assignment is not offered to them, the result is anger, offense and bitterness.

Live It Out

1. What does serving others mean to you?

2. How does serving others take the focus off of your own problems?

3. Name some reasons, or excuses, that might keep you from serving others.

4. Give some examples of "wrong motives" when serving.

5. Name some ways you can remain *available* and *willing* to serve.

Prayer Points

Pray and ask God to show you people and places you can begin to serve today. Get started now, don't wait! You will be so blessed by serving the Lord this way.

Further Study

Read and meditate on the following scriptures.

Scriptures on Serving

Malachi 3:17-18
John 12:26
1 Thessalonians 1:8-10
Hebrews 6:10
Hebrews 9:13-14
Revelation 7:14-15
Matthew 6
Luke 22:27
Romans 12:1
Romans 12:10-11
Ephesians 6:6-8
Acts 20:18-21
Acts 26:6-7
Galatians 5:13
Colossians 3:23-24
1 Peter 1:12

Choose one verse to commit to memory.

Lesson 8
Building Character Through Submission

Oh no, the "S" word! Are you submitted?

A woman of character submits to God. Not just in her head (intellectual) but in her lifestyle.

Submission gets a bad wrap. You might think that to be submitted (to put someone or something above yourself) is to allow yourself to be controlled.
But it is just the opposite....it is freedom! When we are submitted to God, we are therefore to be submitted to our spiritual leaders and teachers, government authority, our spouse and to each other. Healthy submission to your spiritual teachers opens your heart and mind to truly take in what God wants you to learn.

Everyone must submit to governing authorities. For all authority comes from God, and those in positions of authority have been placed there by God. Romans 13:1

He must become greater and greater, and I must become less and less. John 3:30

In the same way, you younger men must accept the authority of the elders. And all of you, serve each other in humility, for "God opposes the proud but favors the humble." So humble yourselves under the mighty power of God, and at the right time he will lift you up in honor. Give all your worries and cares to God, for he cares about you. Stay alert! Watch out for your great enemy, the devil. He prowls around like a roaring lion, looking for someone to devour. Stand firm against him, and be strong in your faith. Remember that your Christian brothers and sisters all over the world are going through the same kind of suffering you are. 1 Peter 5:5-9

"The Christian is under both instruction & authority . . . He believes what he believes because Jesus taught it, and he does what he does because Jesus told him to do it." ~ John Stott

When we submit to God:

- We are teachable. As we submit to God, we put ourselves in the position to learn, to grow and to allow Him to stretch us.
- We are humble. Submitting to God is humbling. It is the recognition of who He is compared to who we are.
- We are flexible. Submitting to God is allowing ourselves to be flexible.
- We submit to one another. God will not promote us until we have shown submission to authority.

What does it mean to submit to God?

First, let me say that submission is often seen as passive. That could not be further from the truth. It actually takes strength to be submissive. When we submit to God, we are giving up control of our lives and allowing God to be the boss. That's not passive, that's brave!

What does it mean to submit to our husband?

For wives, this means submit to your husbands as to the Lord. Ephesians 5:22

Women often ask me how-they can submit to their husband when they know he is less than perfect. Here's how:
We submit to our husbands through our faith in God. This is the Lord's instruction to us and therefore we are to follow. Only through our faith in God are we able to submit in the way God instructs. Our husbands have an equally challenging assignment. They are to love their wives as Jesus loves the Church.

For husbands, this means love your wives, just as Christ loved the church. He gave up his life for her. Ephesians 5:25

Jesus died for the Church. Jesus' example guards against chauvinism and other abuses of the principle of submission.

Submission does not mean:
- A wife does not have independent thoughts.
- A wife does not seek to influence her husband.
- A wife must obey her husband's command to sin.

- A wife is less intelligent or competent than her husband.
- A wife must submit to physical, emotional, mental or spiritual abuse.

Submission does mean:
- A husband and wife are equal with complementary roles, therefore they are mutually submitted.
- Wives are to submit like Jesus did in Gethsemane (Luke 22:42).
- Husbands are to lovingly lead like Jesus does the Church (Eph. 5:25).
- A single woman should only marry a man she can follow.

What about the unbelieving husband?
The bible gives very specific instruction regarding wives of unbelieving husbands:
The same goes for you wives: Be good wives to your husbands, responsive to their needs. There are husbands who, indifferent as they are to any words about God, will be captivated by your life of holy beauty. What matters is not your outer appearance—the styling of your hair, the jewelry you wear, the cut of your clothes—but your inner disposition. 1 Peter 1:4 The Message

Women who have unbelieving husbands should not nag or be preachy, but rather love, serve, and respect their husbands. Their prayers for their husband to accept Christ should never cease and they should continue to honor their spouse daily.

Live It Out

1. What do you think of when you hear the word submission?

2. How does biblical submission connect to being a woman of character?

3. Who do you submit to in your everyday life? (boss, teacher, spouse etc.)

4. What are some of the challenges you face in the area of biblical submission?

5. How does biblical submission relate to being teachable?

Prayer Points

Ask the Lord to reveal any area of your life you have not submitted to Him.
Begin to submit those areas in your life to God.

Further Study
Read and study these verses on submission.

Scriptures on Submission

James 4:7
1 Peter 5:5, 6
Ephesians 5:33
Ephesians 5:21-25, 28
1 Peter 3:1-4
Ephesians 6:5-9
Ephesians 6:1-4
Proverbs 3:5-6
Romans 8:7
1 Peter 5:6
Ephesians 5:21
1 Peter 5:5
 Ephesians 5:22
1 Corinthians 15:28
Romans 13:1
Ephesians 6:5-8

Choose one verse and commit it to memory.

Lesson 9
Building Character Through a Tender Heart

A woman of strong character has a tender, pliable heart and a tenderness of spirit.

Can you tell by looking at someone if their heart is hardened or tender? Not always. A sweet little grandmother can have a hardened heart. A preacher in the pulpit can have a hardened heart. People can have a hardened heart without those closest to them even ever realizing it.

G.D. Watson wrote:

"It is much easier to convince a human soul of its natural impurity than to convince it of its natural hardness, and utter destitution of heavenly and divine tenderness of Spirit. The very essence of the Gospel is a divinely imparted tenderness and sweetness of Spirit. Without this, even the strongest religious life is a misrepresentation of the true Christ-life. Even among intensely religious people, nothing is rarer to find than a continuous, all-pervading spirit of tenderness. It's possible to be very religious, and firm, and persevering in all Christian duties, even to be sanctified, and be a brave defender and preacher of holiness, to be orthodox, and blameless in outward life, and very zealous in good works, and yet to be greatly lacking in tenderness of spirit, that all-subduing, all melting love, which streamed out from the eyes and voice of Jesus.

Many Christians seem loaded with good fruits, but the fruit tastes rotten. There is a touch of vinegar in their sanctity. Their very purity has an icy coldness to it. Their testimonies are straight and definite, but they lack the melting quality. Their prayers are intelligent and strong and pointed, but they lack the heart-piercing pity of the dying Jesus. The summer heat in them is lacking. They preach eloquently and explain with utmost nicety what is actual and original sin and what is pardon and purity, but they lack the burning flame, that interior furnace of throbbing love, that sighs and weeps and breaks down under the shivering heat of all-consuming love."

The Lord sees the condition of our heart. If our heart has a hard shell around it, He wants us to recognize it.

How does a person's heart become hardened? It usually happens a layer at a time. One unhealed, un-forgiven offense or hurt on top of another and another will yield a heart that is crusted over, hardened. It can build up without us knowing it until our behaviour shows up as rebellious, cynical, sarcastic, hateful, or withdrawn.

Our heart can be hardened if we decide to go our own way in spite of what God's word tells us to do.

For the word of God is alive and powerful. It is sharper than the sharpest two-edged sword, cutting between soul and spirit, between joint and marrow. It exposes our innermost thoughts and desires. Hebrews 4:12
If we are not open to receiving the word of God, if we reject it, another layer is formed over our heart.

Read Exodus, chapters 8-10. Here the Bible gives us an account of Pharaoh hearing a message from God and not obeying due to his hardened heart. The Bible says that he hardened his heart and did not listen to the voice of the Lord. His heart was hardened when he decided that he would do something else besides that which God instructed him to do.

If we attend a church service and hear a message on forgiveness but choose to not forgive, we are not receiving God's word. Or, maybe we hear a teaching on tithing, but we continue not to tithe. Both of these are examples of not receiving and obeying the word of God, thus hardening our heart.

In Mark 6:45-52, we read about Jesus sending his disciples across the Sea of Galilee. In the midst of a storm and high winds, Jesus walked to them on the water.

Then he climbed into the boat, and the wind stopped. They were totally amazed, for they still didn't understand the significance of the miracle of the loaves. Their hearts were too hard to take it in. Mark 6:51-52

The disciples had already seen 5,000 people fed with a boy's lunch and there were leftovers! They had seen the evidence of Jesus' miracle power but they didn't understand and "their hearts were too hardened to take it in".

What is the result of a hardened heart? For one thing, when our heart is hardened, we are unable to hear God's voice. We can become insensitive to the voice of God whether it is through the word or hearing in our spirit.

If our heart becomes crusted over we will miss opportunities to reach out and help others. We may miss a chance to share the gospel, to give words of encouragement or come along side someone in trouble.

When you see that your heart has become hardened, repent of the things you have done, or failed to do, that have gotten you into that situation. Commit yourself to faithfully doing what God has told you to do, being grateful for what He's already done for you, and depending on His supernatural power to bless our natural efforts.

Live It Out

1. What kind of person comes to your mind when you think of a person with a hardened heart?

2. Name some of the causes of a hardened heart.

3. Name some of the symptoms of a hardened heart.

4. Why is it important to have a tender and open heart?

Prayer Points
Seek the Lord's guidance regarding the state of your heart. Ask Him to reveal the areas that are not tender and may be hardened.

Further Study
Read Exodus 7-10 Pharaoh's hard heart. Look for evidence that Pharaoh's heart was hardened.
Read the following scriptures on the heart.

Scriptures on the Heart
Ephesians 4:18
Matthew 13:14-15
Proverbs 28:13-14
Hebrews 3:8
Mark 8:17
Exodus 7:3
Jeremiah 17:9
Hebrews 4:12
John 12:48
1 John 3:9
Psalm 119:9
1 Thessalonians 2:13
Genesis 6:5
John 5:39
Philippians 2:13
Ephesians 1:18
1 Peter 5:8
Romans 5:12

Choose one verse to commit to memory.

Lesson 10
Building Character Through Reliability and Loyalty

A woman of character is reliable.

Just say a simple, 'Yes, I will' or 'No, I won't.' Anything beyond this is from the evil one. Matthew 5:37

When is the last time you told someone you would do something and then didn't follow through?

If we make a habit of breaking our promises, we will soon develop a reputation as an unreliable person.

As we read above, in Matthew 5:37, Jesus tells us to say a simple "Yes I will" or "No, I won't." If we say "Yes," but we are consistently unreliable, we do more than damage our own reputation. We damage God's reputation in the eyes of those who see Him through us. Not only can we discourage other Christians, but we may also damage our testimony as Christ followers.

I have never met anyone who really wanted to be known as unreliable. But I have known many women who have too often said "Yes" when they should have said "No." Or, they have said "Yes," but then did not follow through with their commitment.

Occasionally things will come up in our lives that will get in the way of us keeping our commitments. We have all experienced that from time to time. But the person who acquires a reputation for not being reliable will not be trusted and will not reflect the character of Christ.

There are several reasons people become known as unreliable. Sometimes just recognizing the problem and simply making a conscious effort to do what we say we will do will interrupt this cycle. Perhaps improving lack of organization or develop our ability to say "no" will solve this issue.

We can seek God and ask Him for help in taming our calendar and finding His desire for us in terms of organization. It's really okay to devote prayer time to this issue. God cares.

If our struggle involves knowing when or how to say "no," that is what we should address with God.

The bottom line is that unless, and until, we are willing to spend time with God regularly, we probably will not make significant progress in becoming more reliable. And when we you do, we will see significant progress!

It would be easy to overlook punctuality as a problem area. Most people are not happy with being habitually late. We instinctively know that tardiness is bad. In school, many of us were graded on tardiness.

But have you ever stopped to think about what is the result of habitual tardiness might be? Habitual tardiness indicates lack of respect for the other person.

As we work on being women of character who are reliable, we must be aware of any tendency to be late to meetings, appointments, or gatherings of any kind. It shows that we are consistently unreliable. If people expect us to be late, if they plan for us to be late, our reputation is not where we want it.

In effect, we are saying that we consider ourselves more important than those around us. This may sound harsh, but just take a look around a group when someone is habitually late and has that reputation.
Good news! We can overcome this habit and reflect the character of Christ in our actions. We must decide and plan to be early wherever you go.

In other words, allow ourselves margin in planning when we should leave for an event in order to arrive early. Then we must exercise the discipline to leave at that time.

Being reliable is important to us and to God. We must make it a priority. If we want to become known as a reliable person, true to the commitments we make, we must decide to become better organized. We must allow time for listening to God and for personal planning. We must establish routines and commit ourselves to breaking the tardiness habit.

A woman of character is loyal.

Some years ago, I had a very close relationship with a woman from my church community at the time. I believed us to be the type of friends who "had each other's back" and who would remain loyal to each other even through conflict and turmoil. What I discovered is that she was only loyal to me when it worked to her advantage.

Though this experience hurt a great deal, there was a great lesson here for me and I thank God for it. The Lord showed me that loyalty is a character trait. It's a trait that must be developed and while we can't force someone to be loyal to us, we can certainly set the example. If we display loyalty in our lives, we will be an example to our friends and family.

Many of the women I mentor and counsel have much to say on the subject of loyalty. They might not use the specific word, but many relationship issues come down to one thing - loyalty. I believe we are seeing a shift in our culture and a decrease in the importance of being loyal.

So, what does it mean to be loyal? Does it mean sticking by a friend or family member no matter what that person does to you? Does it mean being loyal to a friend only when it fits our needs and is convenient to us? Or does it mean picking and choosing times of loyalty depending on the situation?

As Christ following women, we must explore what it means to be loyal to God in order to understand what it means to be loyal to our family, our friends, our spiritual leaders or our boss.

Being loyal to God

We must never forget what Jesus did for us on the cross. God is loyal to us.

A man of many companions may come to ruin, but there is a friend who sticks closer than a brother. Proverbs 18:24

For the mountains may be removed and the hills may shake, But My loving kindness will not be removed from you, And My covenant of peace will not be shaken," Says the LORD who has compassion on you. Isaiah 54:10

Being loyal to family

Have you heard the saying "You can pick your friends but you can't pick your family?" That expression is meant to say we are "stuck" with the family that God has placed us in. It's true that, typically, we do not choose our family members and we must accept them for who they are. Our treatment of our family should be rooted in Christ. Loyalty in a family is truly accepting our family members for who God made them to be, and remaining loyal to them. What that means is we encourage, support and pray for them. We don't gossip about them, lie about them or set out to hurt them in anyway.

Proverbs 11:29 says: *Whoever troubles his own household will inherit the wind, and the fool will be servant to the wise of heart.*

A wonderful example of family loyalty is found in Ruth, Chapter 1. Ruth was loyal to Naomi, her mother-in-law:

But Ruth said, "Do not urge me to leave you or to return from following you. For where you go I will go, and where you lodge I will lodge. Your people shall be my people, and your God my God. Where you die I will die, and there will I be buried. May the LORD do so to me and more also if anything but death parts me from you." Ruth 1:16-17

Being loyal to friends

1 John 4:20 says *"If people say, "I love God," but hate their brothers or sisters, they are liars. Those who do not love their brothers and sisters, whom they have seen, cannot love God, whom they have never seen."*

This scripture is very specific in its instruction. If we profess to love God, we must love others. I think it is probably safe to say that we have all experienced a breaking of a friendship in some form. Perhaps trust was broken, gossip was spoken or even slander. Betrayal comes in many forms and is all too common. So what does a friendship based on trust and loyalty look like?

Before we can be loyal in a friendship, we must have trust. Trust is built over time and loyalty flows naturally from a trust relationship. A friendship is not always easy. And in fact, in Proverbs we learn that we are to sharpen one another. That might not always be comfortable, but if we trust and are loyal to one another, we make each other better!

Iron sharpens iron, and one man sharpens another. Proverbs 27:17

Demonstrating loyalty

God gauges our heart by how we treat His children. Maintaining a trusting and loyal relationship with our family, friends, spiritual leaders, and bosses honors Him.

So what gets in the way of displaying loyalty? Many times it is un-forgiveness and bitterness. If we harbor un-forgiveness toward a person for any length of time, a root of bitterness can begin to form. From that root of bitterness comes disloyalty.

I recently counseled a woman whose sister had betrayed her in a big way and a huge argument had ensued. Prior to this incident, the two women had been extremely loyal to one another. Even though they pretended that everything was fine between them, they had not forgiven. These two sisters became very disloyal to one another until they finally prayed together and asked God to forgive them and help them forgive. Loyalty between the two was immediately restored!

Our children must be taught loyalty to God, family and friends. Since "more is taught than caught", setting an example for our children is the most effective teaching tool. Teach them to remain loyal to their siblings over siding with friends. Character is formed in the home, therefore we must help our children develop or strengthen this character trait through family interactions.

Live It Out

1. How do you react when a person does not keep their promise to you? What emotions are present?

2. How can being unreliable affect our "witness" to others?

3. What message does a person send when they are habitually tardy?

4. How is loyalty different from friendship? How is it the same as friendship?

5. How do you feel when a friend proves loyal to you?

6. How are you at being a loyal friend?

Prayer Points

Ask the Lord to reveal any areas of your life where you are unreliable or disloyal.

Further Study

Read and study the following scripture references. Choose one to commit to memory.

Scriptures on Reliability and Loyalty

Proverbs 17:17
Matthew 26:33-35
Matthew 26:69-75
Psalm 78:8
Exodus 17:8-13
2 Chronicles 11:13-16
Psalm 84:10-11Proverbs 17:17
Proverbs 18:24
1 Corinthians 16:13-14
Proverbs 21:21
Ruth 1:16-17

Choose one verse to commit to memory.

Lesson 11
Building Character Through Words

Understand this, my dear brothers and sisters: You must all be quick to listen, slow to speak, and slow to get angry. Human anger does not produce the righteousness God desires. So get rid of all the filth and evil in your lives, and humbly accept the word God has planted in your hearts, for it has the power to save your souls. James 1:19-21

We are to listen first, then speak and be slow to anger. You've probably heard the saying that we have 2 ears and 1 mouth for a reason. When we talk more than we listen, we communicate to others that our ideas are more important than theirs. James tells us to reverse the process.

First, we notice that it says to be "quick to listen". To be quick to listen not only means not to start talking when others are, but to also be there to listen when others are going through problems. Or, simply listen because it is polite and kind.

Indeed, we all make many mistakes. For if we could control our tongues, we would be perfect and could also control ourselves in every other way. We can make a large horse go wherever we want by means of a small bit in its mouth. And a small rudder makes a huge ship turn wherever the pilot chooses to go, even though the winds are strong. In the same way, the tongue is a small thing that makes grand speeches. But a tiny spark can set a great forest on fire. James 3:2-5

What we say, and don't say, are both important. Saying the right things at the right time is equally important to not saying things we shouldn't. An uncontrolled tongue includes gossip, bragging, manipulating, tearing others down, lying, complaining, and grumbling. All of these are damaging.

And the tongue is a flame of fire. It is a whole world of wickedness, corrupting your entire body. It can set your whole life on fire, for it is set on fire by hell itself. James 3:6

James compares the damage from the tongue to a fire. Satan uses the tongue to divide people, destroy relationships, and spread destruction within a group. We cannot take back words spoken even with an apology. We can be forgiven, we can apologize, we can repent...but the words are still out there. Nothing can be done to cancel them out. We can however pray that the damage done by our words be neutralized.

Before we speak we should remember that words are like fire—we can neither control them nor reverse the damage. Only God can heal the wounds from words spoken.

People can tame all kinds of animals, birds, reptiles, and fish, but no one can tame the tongue. It is restless and evil, full of deadly poison. James 3:7-8

As human beings we cannot control our tongue on our own. We must allow the Holy Spirit to guide us.

Sometimes it praises our Lord and Father, and sometimes it curses those who have been made in the image of God. And so blessing and cursing come pouring out of the same mouth. Surely, my brothers and sisters, this is not right! Does a spring of water bubble out with both fresh water and bitter water? Does a fig tree produce olives, or a grapevine produce figs? No, and you can't draw fresh water from a salty spring. James 3:9-12

Our speech can either be right and pleasing to God, or destructive and bitter. We must make a choice to bless and not curse with our mouth. We always need the Holy Spirit's help!

A woman of character does not gossip and is aware of the impact of her words.
The dictionary defines gossip as: idle talk or rumor, esp. about the personal or private affairs of others: example *the endless gossip about Hollywood stars.*

Gossip is destructive! Friendships have been destroyed because of gossip. Reputations have been damaged.

A gossip goes around telling secrets, but those who are trustworthy can keep a confidence. Proverbs 11:13

Susie may approach Mary because she trusts her and confides in her on a sensitive, personal subject. Susie has been afraid to share this but decides to trust. Then Mary shares it with Jane who does not know Susie personally. (Enter the third party.) Whether the person who confided knows the trust has been broken does not matter. The friend has broken the trust!

Would you want that trust you have given to someone else broken? I've heard many times "They didn't say I couldn't tell anyone."

Let's get real, if someone has confided in us on a personal or sensitive matter, (finances, relationships, etc.) and they trust us enough to confide in, it should be assumed that it is to remain confidential.

Let's call that implied confidentiality. And the obvious instruction of "please don't share" is explicit.

Here's the thing. No matter what we think our motive is, sharing something that has been told to us in confidence (implied or explicit) is gossip. The only exception is in the case of self-danger, abuse or a life threatening situation. In those cases, we must seek appropriate help.

I am often asked "But what if it is true or seems harmless?" Or, "What if it is about someone that I don't even know?"

The bottom line is, it may not be true. If we didn't personally experience it, or speak with the person it's about, then we don't really know the facts.

Telling lies about others is as harmful as hitting them with an ax, wounding them with a sword, or shooting them with a sharp arrow. Proverbs 25:18

What are axes, swords, or sharp arrows designed to accomplish? They are designed to hurt, destroy, or kill. Do we really want to do these things to another person and better yet, do we want them done to us? Repeating third party gossip is often false testimony. There are always 2 sides to every story and the truth is somewhere in the middle.

Wrongdoers eagerly listen to gossip; liars pay close attention to slander. Proverbs 17:4

Don't listen to gossip, don't listen to slander. Don't believe everything you hear. What is attractive about gossip?

Sometimes knowing what others are doing or are going through takes the focus away from us and our own problems, other times it allows us to judge. There is such danger in gossip I wonder if that danger is attractive to us in some way. Then there is boredom. Sometimes we think it is exciting to hear about what is going on with others.

How do we avoid gossiping?

We must ask the Holy Spirit to make us aware and alert us to gossip. Then we can make the choice not to engage.

When the topic turns to a discussion about a particular person who is not present, don't participate in the conversation.

If we find ourselves a victim of gossip, we aren't to repay an evil act with an evil act of our own.

In Romans 12:19 the Lord says, "It is mine to avenge." The Lord may have us take action in some way, but we should only do that when specifically instructed to do so after prayer.

Live It Out

1. Have you ever been the victim of gossip? What was your reaction? How did you handle the situation?

2. Why do you think people are attracted to gossip?

3. Is it gossip if you are repeating the "facts"?

4. What is the danger in repeating anything you have heard from a 3rd party?

5. What is the best way to avoid being "pulled in" to a gossip situation?

Prayer Points

Repent and ask God for forgiveness for any gossip you have been involved in. Ask Him to help you avoid participating in gossip in the future.

Further Study

Read and meditate on the following verses. Choose one to commit to memory.

Scriptures on Words, Gossip and Slander

Ephesians 4:29
Proverbs 16:28
Proverbs 6:16-19
Proverbs 11:13
Titus 3:2
Proverbs 20:19
Exodus 23:1
James 4:11
Luke 6:31
 James 1:26
Proverbs 26:20
Psalm 101:5
1Timothy 5:13
Proverbs 10:18
Leviticus 19:16
Philippians 1:27
Romans 12:2
Philippians 4:8

Choose one verse to commit to memory.

Lesson 12
Allowing God to Work

"I am the true grapevine, and my Father is the gardener. He cuts off every branch of mine that doesn't produce fruit, and he prunes the branches that do bear fruit so they will produce even more. John 15:1-2

To become women of strong character, we must allow God to prune the dead, destructive behaviors thoughts and actions, patterns of behavior.

Pruning means cutting off to produce good fruit. It hurts or at least is uncomfortable.

However, if we can recognize what pruning is, then it becomes tolerable. We see and understand the necessity and can anticipate what is going to happen as a result.

Where do we start?

Choose to pursue the process of becoming a woman of character.
Free will allows us to choose the path we are going to take. We have free will choices every day.

Get Humble
Remember how the Lord your God led you through the wilderness for these forty years, humbling you and testing you to prove your character, and to find out whether or not you would obey his commands. Deuteronomy 8:2

The Lord tested the children of Israel in the wilderness for forty years— humbled them, tested their character.

Allow God to Work

"I am the true vine, and My Father is the vinedresser. Every branch in Me that does not bear fruit He takes away; and every branch that bears fruit He prunes, that it may bear more fruit. John 15:1-2

Change Our Thinking

Don't copy the behavior and customs of this world, but let God transform you into a new person by changing the way you think. Then you will learn to know God's will for you, which is good and pleasing and perfect. Romans 12:1-2

Changing our thinking will change our behavior. Thoughts=words=actions=outcomes. And actions and outcomes reflect our character.

We must know the fruit we are producing. If it is not glorifying God, then we must be willing to submit to God and allow Him to prune anything that does not glorify Him!

Live It Out

1. How do the verses from John 15:1-2 apply to your life today?

2. Is there an area in your life in which God is pruning you? Name the area and give a specific example of what He is cutting out.

3. What are some reasons we resist being pruned?

4. What are the steps we need to take to allow God to prune areas of our life?

5. What is the reward at the end of this process?

Prayer Points

Ask God to reveal areas of your life that He wants to see change. Then willingly submit to His pruning away of those things.

Further Study

Read and meditate on the following scriptures.

Scriptures on Pruning

Leviticus 25:3-4
Isaiah 5:6
John 15:2
Isaiah 2:4
Isaiah 18:5
Micah 4:3
Joel 3:10
Leviticus 25:3
John 15:2-6
Hebrews 12:6

Choose one verse to commit to memory.

Becoming a Woman of Character
Small Group Leader Guidelines

1. Come to the study prepared. Ask God to help you understand and apply the lesson to your own life.

2. Pray for the women of your group. In order for the lessons to impact the group members, Holy Spirit must be at work in their hearts and lives. Pray for your group members daily.

3. Begin and end on time. Women appreciate punctuality. Begin your meeting on time from day one. Ending the group on time is just as important. Often the women attending your group will have children to pick up or appointments scheduled afterwards.

4. Explain to the group that these studies are meant to be discussions not lectures. Encourage everyone to participate, but realize that some may be hesitant to speak during the first few sessions. Others may participate easily.

5. Try to affirm people's answers whenever possible. The women of your group may be reluctant to speak up at first. Letting them know that you appreciate their thoughts and insight will encourage them to participate. Simple words of affirmation such as "That's a great insight," "Good response," "Excellent idea," or "I hadn't thought of that before" are enough to show people that you value their comments.

6. Don't be afraid of silence. Silence usually seems longer than it really is and often people need time to think about their answer or comment.

7. Resist the temptation to answer your own question. As a leader, you want to avoid doing most of the talking. You may need to rephrase the question or ask it again. The women of your group will want to hear what you have to say but avoid dominating the discussion.

8. Never reject an answer, even if you think it is wrong. When you reject people's answers, it is easy for them to feel rejected as well, and they may decide that it is too risky to give their opinion again. A better response would be to ask them, "Which verse led you to that conclusion?" Or let the group handle the problem by asking them what they think about the question.

9. Avoid wandering. If the discussion wanders off subject, gently bring the group back to the question or scripture being discussed. This is often a big concern with small groups so be firm but kind and bring the subject back to study as quickly as possible.

10. Be aware of the pace. This is a 12 week study. While you won't want to rush your discussions, you will want to stay on task and schedule as much as possible. The goal is to read through the lesson and the questions at a comfortable pace so that you finish at the end of the allotted time. Some lessons will require more discussion time than others. In some situations, you may want to stop and pray for one of your members. Each group will be different.

Snacks/Coffee

The leader/host may want to furnish snacks, coffee or tea or the group may want to rotate bringing a light snack. Be sure to make it clear how that will work at the beginning of the study.

Snacks should be served when the leader thinks best. Some groups serve coffee and snacks on arrival and others serve after study is done. The length of your meeting time can also help determine when snacks are served.

Suggested Timeline

90 minute study-
Greet, pray, worship: 15 minutes
Study/Discussion: 45 minutes
Prayer, snack and chat, clean up: 30 minutes

60 minute study-
Greet and pray: 5 minutes
Study/Discussion: 45 minutes
Prayer, snack and chat, clean up: 10 minutes

NOTES

NOTES

NOTES

NOTES

NOTES

NOTES

NOTES

Made in the USA
San Bernardino, CA
19 August 2015